# SACRED STORY
# YOUTH

# FIRST GRADE

## MY MEDITATION RESPONSE BOOK

# SACRED STORY PRESS

1401 E Jefferson St., STE 405

Seattle, WA 981222

Copyright © 2015 Sacred Story Press

All rights reserved.

ISBN-13: 978-1514320464

ISBN-10: 1514320460

# Dedicated to Our Lady of the Way

Dear Friend:

This is your personal Sacred Story Youth learning log. You are invited to listen to the daily meditations. The SACRED STORY YOUTH meditation quiets your mind so you can hear the voice of God in your heart.

After listening you can write or draw what you thought about during your meditation time. Find a safe and sacred place to keep this learning log.

Sincerely,

Fr. Bill Watson, S.J.

President, President/Founder
Sacred Story Institute

**WEEK**

_____

Grade 1 Learning Log

In the space above draw a picture for Jesus of something for which you are thankful.

God, I love you because

_____.

Jesus, something that makes me sad is

_____.

In the space above draw a picture for Jesus of something for which you are thankful.

God, I love you because

_____ .

Jesus, something that makes me sad is

_____ .

In the space above draw a picture for Jesus of something for which you are thankful.

God, I love you because

_____.

Jesus, something that makes me sad is

_____.

In the space above draw a picture for Jesus of something for which you are thankful.

God, I love you because

_____.

Jesus, something that makes me sad is

_____.

# WEEK

_____

## Grade 1 Learning Log

In the space above draw a picture for Jesus of something for which you are thankful.

God, I love you because

_____.

Jesus, something that makes me sad is

_____.

In the space above draw a picture for Jesus of something for which you are thankful.

God, I love you because

_____ .

Jesus, something that makes me sad is

_____ .

In the space above draw a picture for Jesus of something for which you are thankful.

God, I love you because

_____.

Jesus, something that makes me sad is

_____.

In the space above draw a picture for Jesus of something for which you are thankful.

God, I love you because

_____.

Jesus, something that makes me sad is

_____.

WEEK

_____

Grade 1 Learning Log

In the space above draw a picture for Jesus of something for which you are thankful.

God, I love you because

_____.

Jesus, something that makes me sad is

_____.

# WEEK ____

## Grade 1 Learning Log

In the space above draw a picture for Jesus of something for which you are thankful.

God, I love you because

_____.

Jesus, something that makes me sad is

_____.

In the space above draw a picture for Jesus of something for which you are thankful.

God, I love you because

_____.

Jesus, something that makes me sad is

_____.

## Grade 1 Learning Log

In the space above draw a picture for Jesus of something for which you are thankful.

God, I love you because

_____ .

Jesus, something that makes me sad is

_____ .

**WEEK**

_____

Grade 1 Learning Log

In the space above draw a picture for Jesus of something for which you are thankful.

God, I love you because

_____.

Jesus, something that makes me sad is

_____.

In the space above draw a picture for Jesus of something for which you are thankful.

God, I love you because

_____ .

Jesus, something that makes me sad is

_____ .

# WEEK

_____

## Grade 1 Learning Log

In the space above draw a picture for Jesus of something for which you are thankful.

God, I love you because

_____ .

Jesus, something that makes me sad is

_____ .

# WEEK

_____

## Grade 1 Learning Log

In the space above draw a picture for Jesus of something for which you are thankful.

God, I love you because

_____.

Jesus, something that makes me sad is

_____.

In the space above draw a picture for Jesus of something for which you are thankful.

God, I love you because

_____.

Jesus, something that makes me sad is

_____.

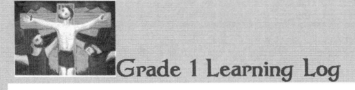

## Grade 1 Learning Log

In the space above draw a picture for Jesus of something for which you are thankful.

God, I love you because

_____.

Jesus, something that makes me sad is

_____.

In the space above draw a picture for Jesus of something for which you are thankful.

God, I love you because

_____.

Jesus, something that makes me sad is

_____.

# WEEK

_____

## Grade 1 Learning Log

In the space above draw a picture for Jesus of something for which you are thankful.

God, I love you because

_____ .

Jesus, something that makes me sad is

_____ .

In the space above draw a picture for Jesus of something for which you are thankful.

God, I love you because

_____ .

Jesus, something that makes me sad is

_____ .

# Grade 1 Learning Log

In the space above draw a picture for Jesus of something for which you are thankful.

God, I love you because

_____ .

Jesus, something that makes me sad is

_____ .

In the space above draw a picture for Jesus of something for which you are thankful.

God, I love you because

_____.

Jesus, something that makes me sad is

_____.

# WEEK

_____

## Grade 1 Learning Log

In the space above draw a picture for Jesus of something for which you are thankful.

God, I love you because

_____.

Jesus, something that makes me sad is

_____.

In the space above draw a picture for Jesus of something for which you are thankful.

God, I love you because

_____ .

Jesus, something that makes me sad is

_____ .

# Grade 1 Learning Log

In the space above draw a picture for Jesus of something for which you are thankful.

God, I love you because

_____.

Jesus, something that makes me sad is

_____.

## Grade 1 Learning Log

In the space above draw a picture for Jesus of something for which you are thankful.

God, I love you because

_____.

Jesus, something that makes me sad is

_____.

In the space above draw a picture for Jesus of something for which you are thankful.

God, I love you because

_____.

Jesus, something that makes me sad is

_____.

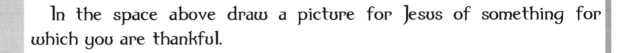
In the space above draw a picture for Jesus of something for which you are thankful.

God, I love you because

_____ .

Jesus, something that makes me sad is

_____ .

In the space above draw a picture for Jesus of something for which you are thankful.

God, I love you because

_____ .

Jesus, something that makes me sad is

_____ .

In the space above draw a picture for Jesus of something for which you are thankful.

God, I love you because

_____.

Jesus, something that makes me sad is

_____.

In the space above draw a picture for Jesus of something for which you are thankful.

God, I love you because

_____.

Jesus, something that makes me sad is

_____.

# WEEK

_____

## Grade 1 Learning Log

In the space above draw a picture for Jesus of something for which you are thankful.

God, I love you because

_____ .

Jesus, something that makes me sad is

_____ .

In the space above draw a picture for Jesus of something for which you are thankful.

God, I love you because

_____.

Jesus, something that makes me sad is

_____.

# WEEK

_____

## Grade 1 Learning Log

In the space above draw a picture for Jesus of something for which you are thankful.

God, I love you because

_____.

Jesus, something that makes me sad is

_____.

In the space above draw a picture for Jesus of something for which you are thankful.

God, I love you because

_____.

Jesus, something that makes me sad is

_____.

# WEEK

_____

## Grade 1 Learning Log

In the space above draw a picture for Jesus of something for which you are thankful.

God, I love you because

_____ .

Jesus, something that makes me sad is

_____ .

# Grade 1 Learning Log

In the space above draw a picture for Jesus of something for which you are thankful.

God, I love you because

_____.

Jesus, something that makes me sad is

_____.

In the space above draw a picture for Jesus of something for which you are thankful.

God, I love you because

_____.

Jesus, something that makes me sad is

_____.

In the space above draw a picture for Jesus of something for which you are thankful.

God, I love you because

_____ .

Jesus, something that makes me sad is

_____ .

In the space above draw a picture for Jesus of something for which you are thankful.

God, I love you because

_____ .

Jesus, something that makes me sad is

_____ .

In the space above draw a picture for Jesus of something for which you are thankful.

God, I love you because

_____ .

Jesus, something that makes me sad is

_____ .

In the space above draw a picture for Jesus of something for which you are thankful.

God, I love you because

_____ .

Jesus, something that makes me sad is

_____ .

In the space above draw a picture for Jesus of something for which you are thankful.

God, I love you because

_____.

Jesus, something that makes me sad is

_____.

In the space above draw a picture for Jesus of something for which you are thankful.

God, I love you because

_____.

Jesus, something that makes me sad is

_____.

In the space above draw a picture for Jesus of something for which you are thankful.


God, I love you because


_____ .


Jesus, something that makes me sad is


_____ .

    In the space above draw a picture for Jesus of something for which you are thankful.

God, I love you because

_____ .

Jesus, something that makes me sad is

_____ .

In the space above draw a picture for Jesus of something for which you are thankful.

God, I love you because

_____ .

Jesus, something that makes me sad is

_____ .

In the space above draw a picture for Jesus of something for which you are thankful.

God, I love you because

_____.

Jesus, something that makes me sad is

_____.

In the space above draw a picture for Jesus of something for which you are thankful.


God, I love you because

_____ .


Jesus, something that makes me sad is

_____ .

In the space above draw a picture for Jesus of something for which you are thankful.

God, I love you because

_____ .

Jesus, something that makes me sad is

_____ .

Grade 1 Learning Log

In the space above draw a picture for Jesus of something for which you are thankful.

God, I love you because

_____.

Jesus, something that makes me sad is

_____.

In the space above draw a picture for Jesus of something for which you are thankful.

God, I love you because

_____ .

Jesus, something that makes me sad is

_____ .

In the space above draw a picture for Jesus of something for which you are thankful.

God, I love you because

_____.

Jesus, something that makes me sad is

_____.

**Sacred Story Institute**
Ignatian Spirituality for Third Millenium Evangelization

1401 E Jefferson
Suite 405
Seattle, WA 98122

Made in the USA
San Bernardino, CA
03 July 2015